FIND YOUR TALENT

START A BLOG!

Matt Anniss

ARCTURUS

This edition first published in 2012 by Arcturus Publishing

Distributed by Black Rabbit Books
P. O. Box 3263
Mankato
Minnesota MN 56002

Printed in China

Library of Congress Cataloging-in-Publication Data

Anniss, Matt.
 Start a blog! / by Matt Anniss.
   p. cm. -- (Find your talent)
 Includes index.
 ISBN 978-1-84858-575-1 (hardcover, library bound)
 1. Blogs. 2. Online journalism. I. Title.
 TK5105.8884.A55 2013
 006.7'52--dc23

2011051448

Text: Matt Anniss
Editors: Joe Harris and Sarah Eason
Design: Paul Myerscough
Cover design: Akihiro Nakayama

Picture credits:
Cover images: Fotolia: Monkey Business Images tc; Shutterstock: Excellent backgrounds br, Germanskydiver ccl, Michael Jung tl, Nina Malyna bl, Monkey Business Images ccr, Alex Nika tr, Photomak cl, Dmitriy Shironosov ct, Piotr Wawrzyniuk bc.
Interior images: Facebook: 26cl; Google: 12c & bl; Joi ItoL: 13tr; Kyle MacDonald: 6bl; Rex Features: NBCUPhotobank 5l; Shutterstock: 1000 Words 27, Yuri Arcurs 21bl, 24-25tc, Arcady 28, africa924 6-7tc, Deepblue-photographer 8-9bc, Darren Brode 4tr, Alias Ching 16-17tc, Arena Creative 16-17bc, Edhar 14b, Helga Esteb 26-27c, Goodluz 11br, Iwona Grodzka 6bl, Martin Haas 9cr, Mat Hayward 8-9tc, Darrin Henry 15b, Dietmar Hoepfl 17bl, Hurricane 22-23tc, Monkey Business Images 19bl, IvincaN5 28-29t, Kak2s 20tr, Keellla 22b, Jan Kranendonk 18b, Montenegro 22-23tc, Olly 10br, Pistolseven 24-25bc, Pix2go 4br, Cosmin-Constantin Sava 22bc, Selena 5tr, 21tr, Sheff 13bl, Dmitriy Shironosov 1, Luboslav Tiles 15cl, Petr Vaclavek 10tr, Visiva 23bl; Wordpress: 12b.

Every attempt has been made to clear copyright. Should there be any inadvertent omission, please apply to the publisher for rectification.

SL002141US
Supplier 03 Date 0412 Print run 1451

CONTENTS

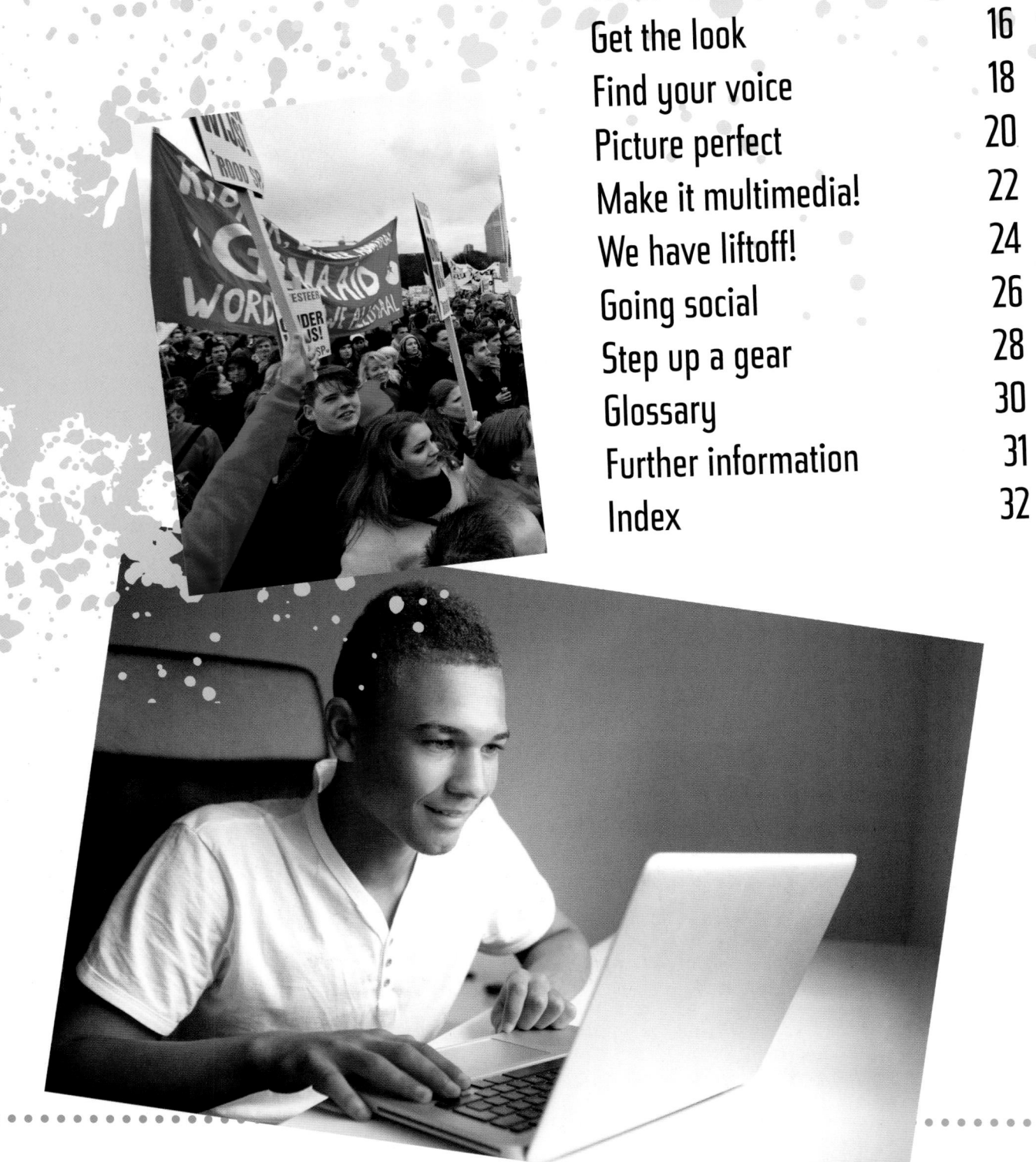

FIND YOUR TALENT!

Around the world, thousands of people are writing about things that excite, inspire, delight, or frustrate them. They share their thoughts at the click of a mouse button. They are called bloggers.

Blogging dreams Anyone can be a blogger. If you have a passion for a particular subject, cause, or activity, you have what it takes to be a blogger. Blogs can be about anything and everything—there are no set rules. Your blog is your space to do whatever you want, whether that is collecting funny pictures, reviewing the latest bands and singers, or writing about your favorite football team.

The journey begins The main purpose of a blog is to give a voice to anyone with a computer. Thanks to online blogging software, you do not need to know how to design a web site. All you need is a bagful of ideas, a passion for your ideas, and to be willing to update your blog regularly.

Many blogs feature funny or quirky pictures. If you make your readers smile, they will be back for more!

Blogger Neil Pasricha found worldwide fame by writing about "awesome" things that excite him.

Many bloggers write about popular sports and hobbies such as cycling.

Let's go! Across the next few pages, we will explain how you can go about starting your own blog. We will reveal the real-life stories behind some of the biggest blogs on the Internet, and show you how your blog can be a success with a mix of hard work and great ideas.

INSIDE STORY: AWESOME

Neil Pasricha started his 1000 Awesome Things blog in 2008. "The blog was meant to be that one little place where we turn the lights out, put a blanket over our heads and just talk about popping bubble wrap, snow days, or the smell of a bakery," he explained. Since then, Neil has written about a different "awesome" thing every day. In doing so, he has picked up thousands of fans, written two best-selling books, and won many awards.

WELCOME TO THE BLOGOSPHERE!

If you typed the word "blog" into a search engine, you would get thousands of results. That is because the Internet is jam-packed with millions of blogs. If your blog is to be a success, you need to find something special to write about.

Blogs can be used to campaign for change and highlight important issues such as Third World hunger.

Pick a subject If you picked a topic at random, from nuclear physics to sticker collecting, there would almost certainly be at least one blog about it. Don't worry if your favorite subject is already covered—in the blogosphere, there is room for everyone! Your blog can be about anything, as long as it matters to you.

Blogs don't have to be serious—they can be fun, too! Your blog could be about sock puppets, soccer, or shoes. You're the boss!

Blog on! Blogs come in many shapes and sizes. Some people use their blogs to campaign about particular issues, such as the environment. Others use their blogs as personal diaries, sharing their highs and lows with the world. Some blogs offer information about news events. There are funny blogs, too, designed to make their readers smile. In the blogosphere, anything goes!

Canadian Kyle MacDonald traded his way from a single red paper clip to a brand new house—all via his blog.

EARLY DAYS: Kyle MacDonald

Sometimes, the best ideas for blogs are the simplest. Canadian Kyle MacDonald was 23 when he decided to try to swap his way to a house. Setting up his own blog, he first offered to trade a red paper clip. A year and 14 trades later, he was the proud owner of his first home!

BLOGGING FOR BEGINNERS

To make your blog stand out, you first need to discover which key features make a great blog.

Reviews of live performances and new CDs are a popular feature of many music blogs.

Blog best bits Blogs are really quite simple. Although they can be developed into web sites with many sections, most of the best blogs have a homepage that showcases entries or posts. These can be short pieces with links to interesting web sites, videos or music tracks, or long interviews, reports, and reviews. Each post has its own title to attract readers. It also usually features a short paragraph to draw people in, and something else to read, look at, or listen to.

EARLY DAYS: Worldwide hit

Now famous around the world, The Huffington Post attracts 54 million visits every year. However, the blog wasn't always this popular. Founder Arianna Huffington was already a successful writer when she decided to try her hand at blogging in 2005. Her idea was to create a blog that would double as an Internet-only newspaper. With its busy homepage and plenty of posts, The Huffington Post quickly became a worldwide hit.

One of the biggest tasks facing any blogger is coming up with lots of ideas for posts. Here are some helpful tips:

- Before you plan your blog in detail, brainstorm or write down possible posts for your blog.
- Think about your chosen subject and see if you can come up with ten ideas to write about.

Storms caused by global warming would make an interesting topic for an environmental news blog.

Blogs can be used to promote your skills and interests, whether you're into dancing or demonstrations.

Perfect posts The world's most successful blogs are updated often. Some offer new posts every day, others weekly updates or articles that pop up every few days. You might not have time to write something new on your blog every day. However, if you are going to attract readers, you will need to make sure you keep posting. Regular posts keep readers coming back time and time again.

WHAT'S THE PLAN?

Many people decide to start blogs on a whim and as a result give up quite quickly. If your blog is going to attract readers, you will need to have a clear structure.

Home is where the heart is The heart of any blog is the homepage. Most advertise the other pages and sections of a blog that will be of interest to readers. It is these extra sections that can turn a good blog into a really great blog.

All about... If you look at popular blogs, you will often find an "About" page. This part of the blog may link to web sites, audio, and video sections. It may also have picture galleries and a "contact" page where readers can email the author. You will need to decide which of these features you want to include.

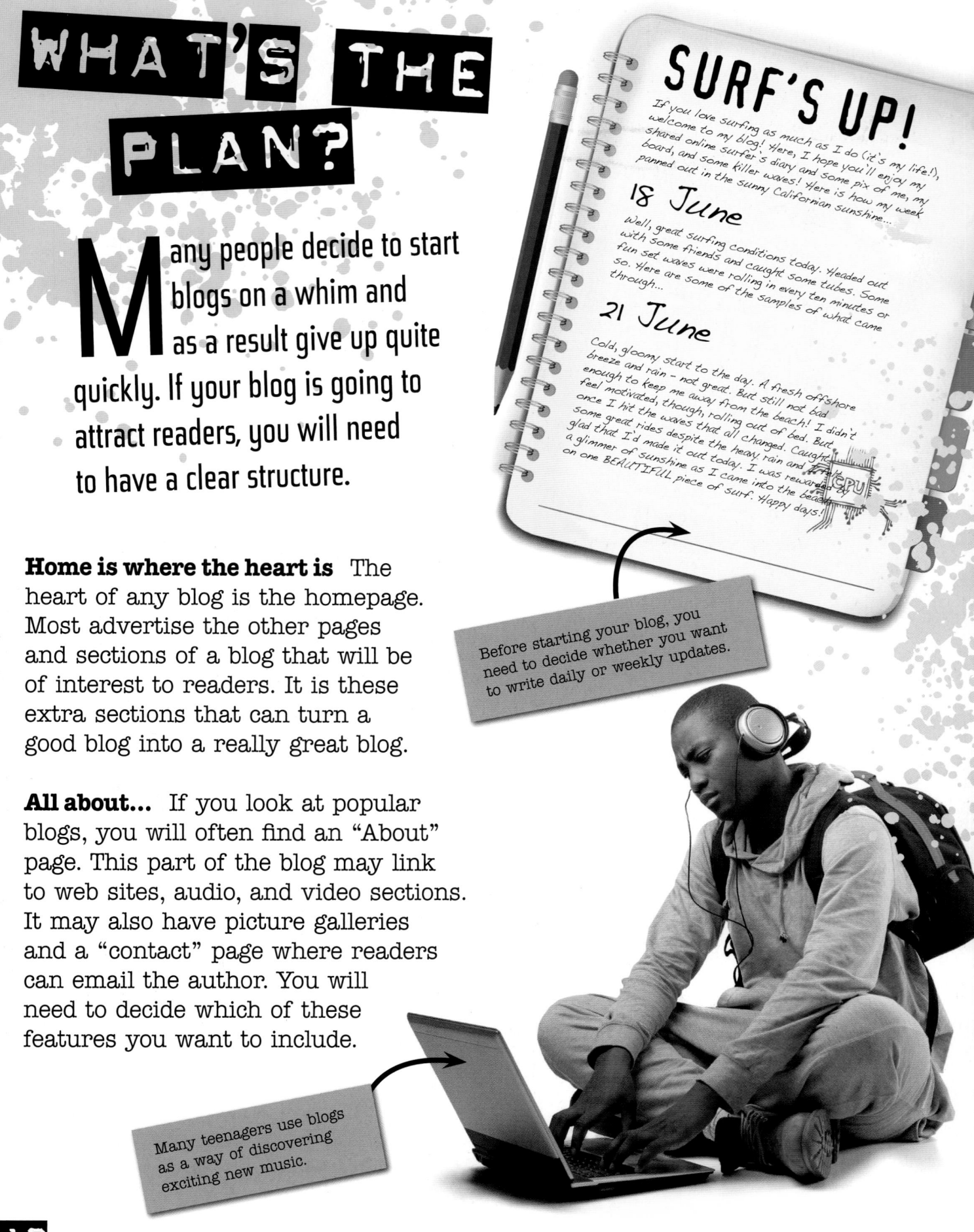

SURF'S UP!

If you love surfing as much as I do (it's my life!), welcome to my blog! Here, I hope you'll enjoy my shared online surfer's diary and some pix of me, my board, and some killer waves! Here is how my week panned out in the sunny Californian sunshine...

18 June

Well, great surfing conditions today. Headed out with some friends and caught some tubes. Some fun set waves were rolling in every ten minutes or so. Here are some of the samples of what came through...

21 June

Cold, gloomy start to the day. A fresh offshore breeze and rain – not great. But still not bad enough to keep me away from the beach! I didn't feel motivated, though, rolling out of bed. But once I hit the waves that all changed. Caught some great rides despite the heavy rain and glad that I'd made it out today. I was rewarded a glimmer of sunshine as I came into the beach on one BEAUTIFUL piece of surf. Happy days!

Before starting your blog, you need to decide whether you want to write daily or weekly updates.

Many teenagers use blogs as a way of discovering exciting new music.

INSIDE STORY: GOING UNDERGROUND

Would-be journalist Tony Poland set up his Slutty Fringe blog in 2009. The blog featured music, fashion, and art. Tony soon found it hard to update the web site every day, so he looked for writers to help him. Six of his friends got involved, and now the blog is one of the most popular underground music sites around.

Helping hands You should also think about whether you want to get friends to help with your blog. Having a number of writers can allow the blog to be updated more often, which can attract more readers.

Many of the world's best blogs are written by groups of friends.

GO FOR IT: THE MASTER PLAN

Sketch out the plan for your blog:
- Draw a square, circle, or rectangle to represent your blog's homepage.
- Add any other sections you want to feature on your blog. Draw them around the homepage image. Use smaller circles, rectangles, or squares to represent different pages.
- Draw lines to connect all the smaller pages to the homepage image.

START IT UP

f you are almost ready to start making your blog, the very next step is to find some space on the Internet to host it. Sounds daunting? It's easy when you know how...

The host with the most All web sites, including blogs, have a host. This is usually a company that stores the site's information on a computer called a server. The most popular blog hosts in the world are Google's Blogger, Tumblr, and WordPress.

Step-by-step Once you've chosen a host, the next step is to pick your blog name. After that, you'll sign up for a free account. Your host will then explain step-by-step how to create your blog. All the information you need to know will be included, from writing an "About" page to posting your first blog entry. Host sites allow you to design, write, and manage your blog online. They provide a set of tools to format text, enter web links, and upload pictures.

Take some time to choose your host, whether it's Blogger, Tumblr, or WordPress.

EARLY DAYS: The first blogger

In 1994, the Internet was still very young. It was back then that Swarthmore College student Justin Hall decided to create his own online diary. Titled Justin's Links, it initially featured lists of interesting web sites. Justin soon found himself telling site visitors about his daily life in a "web log"—the name was later shortened to blog! It took a long time for blogging to really take off, so Justin was a true pioneer.

While there are now millions of blogs, Justin Hall's was the very first.

Signing up with a blog host is easy and only takes a few minutes.

GO FOR IT: YOUR FIRST BLOG

It is now time to create your blog:
- Sign up with a blog-hosting web site such as Blogger, Tumblr, or WordPress.
- Go to your chosen web site, find the "get started" button, and follow the instructions.
- Enter your name and email address, choose a password (so no one else can change your blog without your permission). Pick both a name and web address for your new blog.
- Press "submit." You are now the proud owner of your first blog!

WHAT IS IT ALL ABOUT?

The success of the "Word of the Day" blog proves that simple ideas are often the best.

If you are going to attract new readers to your blog, your homepage will need to explain exactly what your blog is about. This is your mission statement. It will show what viewers can expect to see on your blog over the coming weeks, months, and years.

All "About" the blog The best way to tell would-be readers about your blog is to create a permanent page or post. This is called the "About" page. It is here that your mission statement will appear, and where you can tell readers about yourself and your writers. The About page will be one of the first sections read by visitors to your blog.

INSIDE STORY: WORD OF THE DAY

Some blogs are so simple they really don't need a mission statement. Word of the Day offers a dictionary explanation of an odd or interesting word every day. Creator Natalie's About page is simple, short and sweet: "I'm French. I live in Italy. Anything else you think you might need to know about me, you will have to invent!"

From the heart The About section of your blog is your first chance to show would-be readers that you have both passion and personality. In a few sentences or paragraphs, you can tell people about yourself and your blog. This is your chance to impress and tell the world why your blog matters, so be enthusiastic!

Writing your "About" page allows you to set the scene for your readers.

GO FOR IT: LOOK AT ME!

Follow these steps to write an attention-grabbing About page:
- Make sure you are happy with your mission statement before posting it on your blog.
- Keep it short and sweet—roughly a paragraph or two at the most.
- Include information about yourself and the blog.
- When you are happy with what you have written, log in to your chosen blogging site and try posting it to your blog.
- If you are unsure about what to do, all blogging sites have great "help" sections. These usually include step-by-step instructions and tutorial videos.

The best bloggers engage readers by putting some of their personality into their writing.

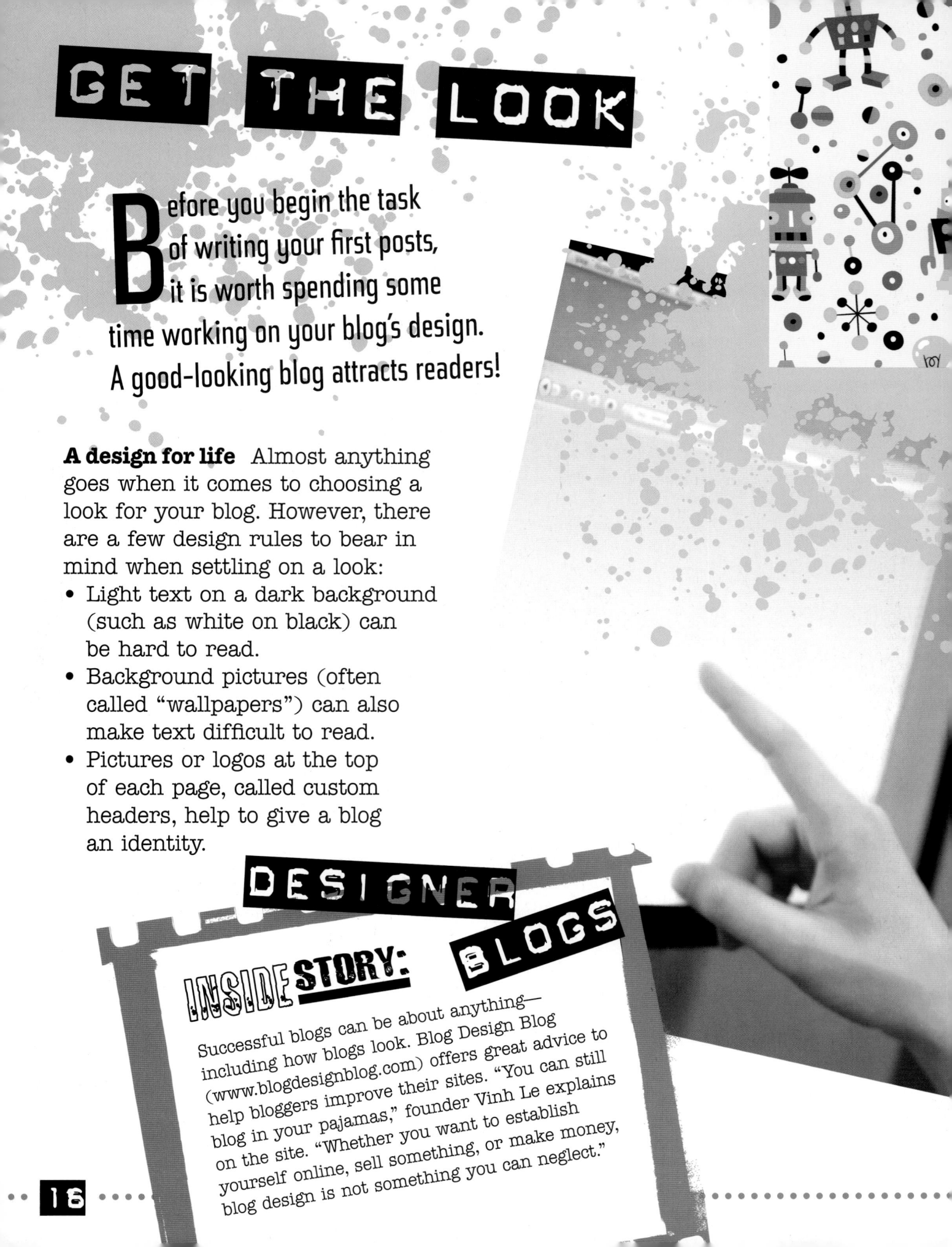

GET THE LOOK

Before you begin the task of writing your first posts, it is worth spending some time working on your blog's design. A good-looking blog attracts readers!

A design for life Almost anything goes when it comes to choosing a look for your blog. However, there are a few design rules to bear in mind when settling on a look:

- Light text on a dark background (such as white on black) can be hard to read.
- Background pictures (often called "wallpapers") can also make text difficult to read.
- Pictures or logos at the top of each page, called custom headers, help to give a blog an identity.

INSIDE STORY: DESIGNER BLOGS

Successful blogs can be about anything—including how blogs look. Blog Design Blog (www.blogdesignblog.com) offers great advice to help bloggers improve their sites. "You can still blog in your pajamas," founder Vinh Le explains on the site. "Whether you want to establish yourself online, sell something, or make money, blog design is not something you can neglect."

Sweet themes To take the hard work out of designing your blog, the major blogging sites have "themes." These are design templates you can use for free and change to suit your blog. There are hundreds of different themes to choose from. Each has different colors, slightly different layouts, and lots of fonts. Some themes are simple, others are more complicated. Some have lots of pictures, whereas others have more text. All have been designed to make blogs look GREAT!

You could brighten up the look of your blog by using specially designed backgrounds called "wallpapers."

GO FOR IT: WHAT'S YOUR THEME?

Some handy tips for choosing a great blog design:
- Check out all the available themes before making a decision.
- Try a few themes before you choose your favorite one.
- "Apply" the theme to your blog.

Because it's the first thing that people see, it's always worth taking a closer look at the design of your blog.

There are hundreds and thousands of icons that can be used to make your blog stand out.

FIND YOUR VOICE

By now, you should be itching to write your first-ever blog post! Before you start, it is worth taking a little time to think about your writing style. If your blog is going to be a success, you will need to find your voice.

Talking your language

Writing is very personal and language can be used in many different ways. It can be funny, touching, hard-hitting, informative, or imaginative. The best bloggers use some or all of these styles in their writing. They also vary the length of their sentences to give their posts pace.

These students held a demo to get their point across—you can get the same result by writing on your blog.

INSIDE STORY: WRITE ON!

Tina Su set up her blog Think Simple Now in 2007. Within three months, she'd picked up well over 2,000 subscribers. "I obsess over my writing," she says. "I feel responsible for my readers and want to give them the best quality I can produce. Try different writing styles to test out which your readers respond to most."

Style up! If you are unsure of your voice or style, read a few blogs to find out how other bloggers write. Try not to copy them, though—your writing style should show your personality.

Short and sweet Blog visitors very rarely read long articles, so it is important to make your posts short and snappy. Start by hooking in your readers with a great opening sentence. Then continue with short, easy-to-read paragraphs. Make your point in as few words as possible, and in your own style. Keep it up and you will soon be on the way to being a great blogger.

The best bloggers all develop their own unique writing style to stand out from the crowd.

GO FOR IT: FIRST POST

The moment you've been waiting for has arrived—it's time to write your first blog post!

- Choose a subject close to your heart—something you know about or have strong opinions about.
- Log in to your blog, click on "new post," and start writing.
- Keep your post short, to-the-point, and interesting.
- When you have finished, choose a headline and check through for spelling mistakes.
- Save your post as a draft (for now!).

PICTURE PERFECT

You have designed your blog, told people what it is all about, and written your first post. Now, it is time to add pictures. Whether you take photos yourself or find them elsewhere, pictures are an important part of any great blog.

Using striking images like this one can really bring your blog to life.

Image is everything Pictures make blog posts easier to read. This might seem a bit strange at first, but have you ever tried to read a blog that just contains pages of text and no images? It really is not that easy. While it may be readable, it will feel a bit dull!

INSIDE STORY: JUST FOR GIRLS

Many great blogs focus solely on photography. Tracey Clark set up the Shutter Sisters blog to showcase great pictures taken just by women. "We're committed to honoring the beauty women behind a camera can capture," Tracey explains on the site.

Size matters There are a number of ways to add images to a blog post. The first is to take your own pictures and upload them to your blog. The second is to find the image you want on the Internet and then use the image's web address to copy it into your post. If you are taking your own pictures, you will need to make sure that they are the right file format and size—JPEGs at 72 dpi (dots per inch) are best.

Creating your own illustrations can help give your blog its unique visual identity.

GO FOR IT: ADD A PICTURE

Remember the first blog post you saved as a draft? We're now going to add a photo to it:

- Take a picture.
- Download it onto your computer and note down where it is saved.
- On your blogging web site, open up the draft post you saved.
- Click on the "picture" icon in the tool bar (it usually looks like a box or tiny painting).
- Follow the instructions to add your picture.
- Click on "submit post" or "post."
- Your first-ever blog post should now be live!

Making a good first impression is vital. That's why photos are so important to blogs.

MAKE IT MULTIMEDIA!

The best blogs do not rely only on the quality of their writing and pictures to attract readers. Smart bloggers know that including multimedia content, such as videos and music, is a great way to gain new visitors.

Get "vlogging!" Some bloggers prefer to share their thoughts on a subject using homemade video clips. This is referred to as "vlogging" (from "video blogging"). Some blogs use both homemade vlog posts and articles, while others link to videos they've found elsewhere online, such as on YouTube.

If you've ever dreamed of making your own short TV shows, you should try video blogging, sometimes referred to as "vlogging."

Many bedroom DJs showcase their skills by posting mixes to their personal blogs.

- In 2007, Peter Rojas had a great idea. He decided to start a blog on which people could share free MP3s of the best new music around. He joined forces with a music company and offered his idea to record companies. His RCRD LBL blog was born and bands soon offered him tracks to give away free. The blog is now one of the most popular music blogs on the Internet.

Record labels take a dim view of bloggers who illegally upload MP3 music files to their blogs.

Feel the music Music can be shared in a similar way to video clips, and is also very popular with bloggers and their visitors. Homemade radio-style podcasts and DJ mixes are featured on many music blogs.

Free sounds Some bands even give their music away for free through blogs. Music web sites such as SoundCloud and Mixcloud allow bloggers to share music. Important! Do not upload MP3 tracks from your own music collection! This is illegal.

GO FOR IT: AND UPLOAD!

Now it is time to add video to your blog:

- Film a video clip you'd like to show on your blog on a digital camera or cell phone.
- Transfer the clip to your computer. Make a note of where you saved the film file.
- Log in to your blog and begin a new post.
- Look at the host site's tool bar. You should see a button for adding videos—it looks like a picture of a video camera.
- Click on the button and follow the instructions to add a video.

23

WE HAVE LIFTOFF!

Now that you have mastered blogging basics, your new blog is almost ready for launch. Just hold off a little longer! It is worth taking some time to make sure your blog is exactly right before telling the world about it.

Practice makes perfect Practice your blogging skills before "going live." Most blogging sites offer the option to make your posts "private," which means no one can see them unless you allow them to. This helps you to easily correct mistakes before you go live.

INSIDE STORY: LAUNCH DAY

Lachy G, an Australian teenager, has been making blogs since he was 11. His most successful blog to date is Uncoverr.com, which offers reviews of books for web site designers. The site is now very popular, but that wasn't always the case. "I planned the launch pretty badly," Lachy said in 2011. "I was expecting 5,000 visitors on the first day, but it was more like 1,000. I should have got a lot more posts done before launching."

Before promoting your blog to the world, you could text your friends to let them know about the site.

Private view When you are just about ready to launch, invite your friends to take a look at your blog and offer feedback. This is vital because it gives you time to make any essential alterations before launch day.

Going public Once you are happy that your blog is perfect, you are ready to turn it from "private" to "public." It's time to announce your brand-new web site to the world! When you have launched, do not be disheartened if feedback is slow to come. It can take some bloggers years to build up a following. Remember, this is just the start of your journey!

If you make your blog "private" to begin with, your friends can offer vital feedback before it goes "public."

GO FOR IT: SPREAD THE WORD

Now your blog has launched, you need to tell the world about it. There are loads of different ways to do this:

- Email or text your friends to let them know about your blog.
- Put up ads on your school notice boards.
- Post details of your new blog on Internet forums and message boards.

GOING SOCIAL

The success of your blog depends not just on the quality of your content, but also on the number of regular visitors to your site. To make sure enough people visit your blog, you need to market it. One of the best ways to do that is through social networks such as Facebook and Twitter.

Interest in the lives of stars such as Emma Watson has helped make celebrity blog TMZ a massive success.

facebook

Many bloggers successfully promote their posts through social media sites such as Facebook.

Networking Social networking web sites can be great places to tell everyone about your blog. Most bloggers post web links to their articles on social networks that tell friends and family about new features. Many bloggers start "pages" and "groups" on Facebook to help attract new readers.

GO FOR IT: TELL EVERYONE!

One of the best ways to use Facebook is to start a "page" to promote your blog. If people "like" your page, they will automatically see these updates. To start a page, follow these steps:

- Log into Facebook and scroll to the bottom of the screen.
- Click on the "create a page" link and follow the instructions.
- You will need to tell people a little bit about your blog and include a picture. This is your chance to sell your site, so be creative!

INSIDE STORY: TMZ

Entertainment gossip web site TMZ launched in 2005 and has since become a huge success story. The blog became famous for posting stories about Hollywood celebrities before newspapers could get hold of them. The blog is now visited more than 19 million times a month, making it one of the most-read sites on the Internet. TMZ uses Twitter to attract readers by posting teasing snippets of its latest news stories.

Tweet style Another great blog promotion tip is "microblogging." This offers an opportunity to post short summaries of your new blog posts on sites such as Twitter. The posts are sent to "followers." Many blog providers now offer Twitter and Facebook integration. This means your articles can be shared on microblogging sites and social networks the moment you click "post."

Microblogging sites such as Twitter help bloggers interact directly with their readers.

STEP UP A GEAR

You have joined the thousands of bloggers around the world! Now, there are plenty of ways you can develop and improve your blog in the months and years ahead...

Build a community Some of the best blogs around the world have a real community feel, with bloggers and their readers regularly "talking" online. To build a community, ask people to comment on your posts or offer regular visitors a chance to write articles. Both are excellent ways to get other people involved in your blog!

Post polls Most blogging services allow you to add polls to your site. These are sections in which visitors can vote for something. It could be the latest album by your favorite band, a big news story, or whether a new film is good or bad.

Start a podcast series
Podcasts are short audio or video programs. They can be in the style of radio shows, DJ mixes, TV news reports, or comedy showcases. People can download and listen to podcasts. They can also watch them on their computers, media players, or cell phones.

Many blogs offer regular podcasts because they give visitors a great reason to keep returning. People can subscribe to podcasts using software such as iTunes, which will then automatically download new episodes for them.

Interviewing people in the news can attract thousands of new readers to your blog.

Interview people Another popular feature of many blogs are question-and-answer style interviews. Young bands, sports people, actors, and artists will often agree to be interviewed by bloggers. If you email their manager or PR representative, you might be lucky enough to get an interview. Celebrity interviews are a great way to attract readers to your blog.

Mix up your content You can write about almost anything on a blog, in many different styles. This means you can include all sorts of information. For example, you could report from a big playoff game, or write news stories about interesting things happening in your area. You could even review new TV shows, movies, or music releases. The possibilities are endless!

GLOSSARY

articles interesting pieces of writing about something

audio something that is heard

awards prizes

bloggers slang term for people who create blogs

blogosphere popular term used to describe the global blogging community

brainstorm writing down a lot of different ideas

campaign when a group of people work together to try to change something

cause something people believe strongly in

community a number of people who share common interests or live close to each other

draft a first attempt at something, such as a draft letter

file format a type of file, for example, a picture or piece of music

fonts different styles of typed letters

format to change something so it fits a consistent style

free account an online account with a web site that you do not need to pay for

headline the large words at the top of a page that tell you what it is about

homepage the first page of a web site

honoring showing respect

host Internet term for storing a web site

identity a look or personality associated with someone or something

JPEG a type of file format for storing pictures digitally on a computer

layouts page designs

links web site addresses

log in to sign in to something with a particular name and password

market to make people aware of a product or service

microblogging a term used to refer to sites such as Twitter, which allow you to post very short messages

mission statement an explanation of your aims

neglect to not take care of something

online any activity on the Internet

pace the speed at which something moves

picture galleries places online, such as on a blog, where images can be seen

pioneer one of the first people to do something

poll a system that shows how many people have voted for something

posting sending messages online

posts messages sent online

reports written pieces that tell people about something, such as a news event

reviewing writing your opinion about something

search engine a system on the Internet that searches for information for you

server a central place on the Internet where information is stored

showcase to show something off

software computer programs

structure the organization and design of something

subscribe to pay for something regularly

templates designs that can be used over and over again

tutorial a lesson

underground not mainstream

updated kept up-to-date

upload to put something on the Internet

FURTHER INFORMATION

Books

Blogging for Dummies, by Susannah Gardner and Shane Birley (Wiley & Sons, 2010)

Blogging Heroes: Interviews with 30 of the World's Top Bloggers, by Michael A. Banks (Wiley & Sons, 2007)

Creating Your First Blog: 6 Easy Blogging Projects to Start Blogging Like a Pro, by Tris Hussey (Sams, 2010)

The Huffington Post Complete Guide to Blogging (Simon & Schuster, 2009)

One Red Paperclip, by Kyle MacDonald (Ebury Press, 2008)

The Rough Guide to Blogging, by Jonathan Yang (Rough Guides, 2006)

Web Sites

Best Blogging Tips Online
Read great top tips from experienced bloggers:
www.bestbloggingtipsonline.com

Blogger
The original online blogging service, used by millions of people worldwide:
www.blogger.com

ProBlogger
Find out how to make money from your blog:
www.problogger.com

Tumblr
A popular online blogging service that will host your blog for free:
www.tumblr.com

Twitter
Check out the world's most popular "microblogging" site:
www.twitter.com

WordPress
One of the world's most popular blogging services, hosting hundreds of thousands of free blogs:
www.wordpress.com

Apps

BloggerPlus
No computer? No problem—this iPhone app lets you create a blog direct from your phone!

BlogPress
Update your blog and social network profiles on the go, direct from your iPhone or iPad.

WordPress
Available on both iPhone and Android, this app allows you to update your WordPress blog wherever you are in the world.

INDEX